TIME FOR KIDS READERS

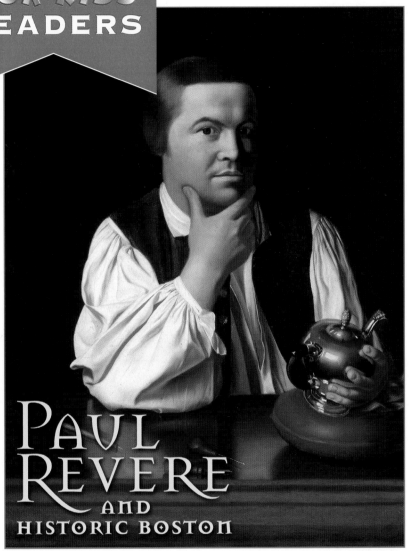

PAUL REVERE

AND

HISTORIC BOSTON

by Susan Ring

Harcourt

Orlando   Austin   Chicago   New York   Toronto   London   San Diego

Visit *The Learning Site!*
www.harcourtschool.com

Paul Revere was born in Boston in 1735. He worked there as a silversmith. He also helped America become a free nation.

This statue of Paul Revere stands near the Old North Church.

Paul Revere felt that the British had made unfair laws for the colonies. At meetings, he talked about how the colonists could make things better.

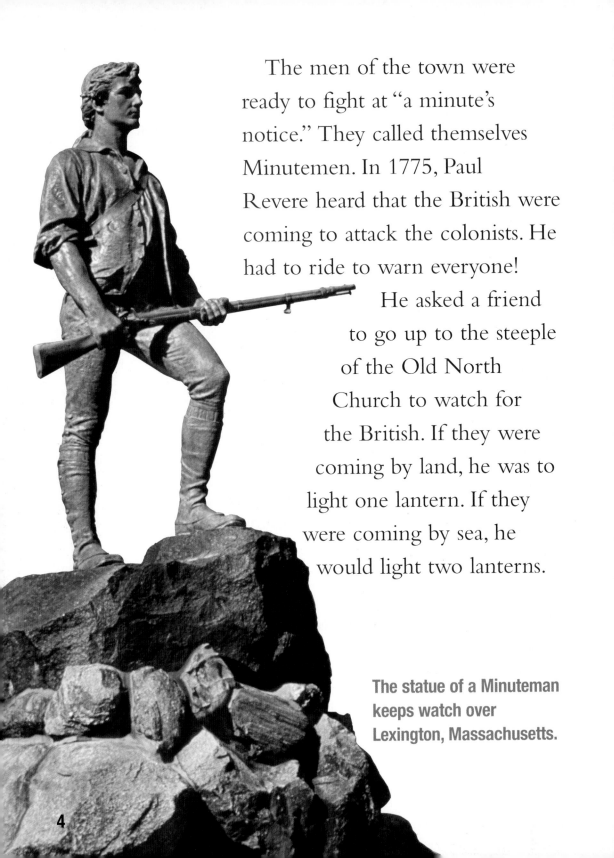

The men of the town were ready to fight at "a minute's notice." They called themselves Minutemen. In 1775, Paul Revere heard that the British were coming to attack the colonists. He had to ride to warn everyone!

He asked a friend to go up to the steeple of the Old North Church to watch for the British. If they were coming by land, he was to light one lantern. If they were coming by sea, he would light two lanterns.

The statue of a Minuteman keeps watch over Lexington, Massachusetts.

In 1775, two lanterns shone from the steeple of the Old North Church.

When Paul Revere saw two lanterns shining, he rode his horse for many miles. He told everyone that British troops were coming. Because of this warning, the Minutemen were ready.

After the Revolutionary War, Paul Revere still helped Boston. People did not want to use British money anymore, so he printed new money. In 1803, his mill made the sheets of copper for the roof of the first State House. He also made copper nails and spikes that were used to build ships.

This is the State House today. Gold was placed over the copper dome in 1874.

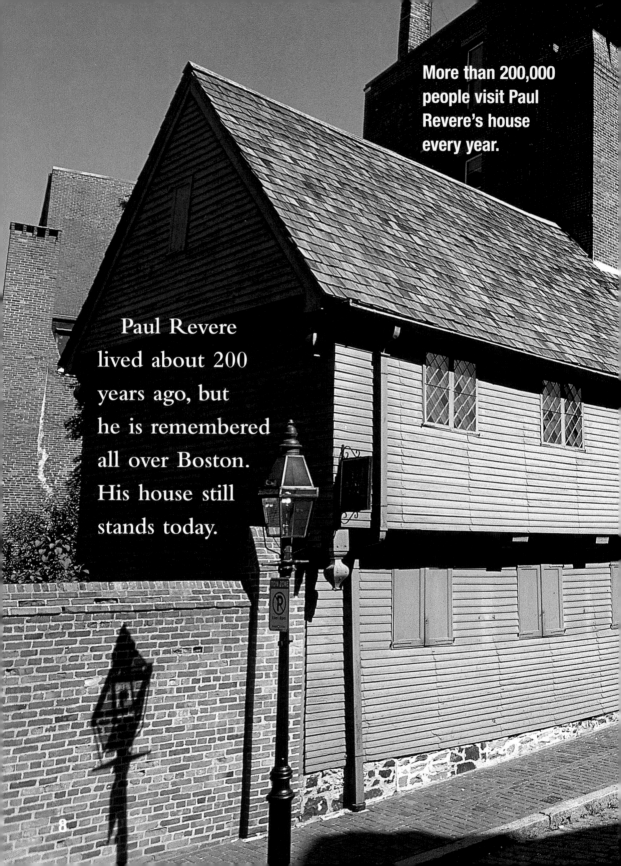

More than 200,000 people visit Paul Revere's house every year.

Paul Revere lived about 200 years ago, but he is remembered all over Boston. His house still stands today.